Discovering Religions

Christianity

Sue Penney

D0320162

Heinemann Educational Publishers
Halley Court, Jordan Hill, Oxford OX2 8EJ

MADRID ATHENS PARIS
FLORENCE PRAGUE WARSAW
PORTSMOUTH NH CHICAGO SAO PAULO
SINGAPORE TOKYO MELBOURNE AUCKLAND
IBADAN GABORONE JOHANNESBURG

First published 1987
Revised edition published 1995

99 98 97 96 95
10 9 8 7 6 5 4 3 2

British Library Cataloguing in Publication Data
A catalogue record for this book is available from the British Library

ISBN 0 435 30466 6

Designed and typeset by Visual Image
Illustrated by Gecko limited. Adapted into colour by Visual Image
Produced by Mandarin Offset
Printed and bound in China

Acknowledgements
Thanks are due to our Religious Studies consultant, W Owen Cole, for reading and
advising on the manuscript.

The author and publishers would like to thank the following for permission to use
photographs:
The Ancient Art and Architecture Collection p. 35; Andes Press Agency pp. 7,
9 (right), 16 (both), 20, 21 (left); The Bridgeman Art Library pp. 23, 24; Paul Bryans
p. 14 (right); Cambridge Evening News p. 44 (top); Circa Photo Library p. 46;
C M Dixon p. 33; Keith Ellis pp. 21 (right), 42; Mary Evans Picture Library p. 34;
Glasgow Museums: the St Mungo Museum of Religious Life and Art p. 27; Sally and
Richard Greenhill p. 43, 44 (below); Sonia Halliday Photographs pp. 17, 25, 30, 31;
Robert Harding Picture Library p. 9 (left); J Allan Cash Photo Library pp. 6, 15, 40, 47;
Network Photographers pp. 8, 36; Philip Parkhouse p. 38; Ann and Bury Peerless
p. 39; Frank Spooner Pictures p. 11; Simon Warner p. 19; Zefa pp. 10, 13, 14 (left),
41.

The publishers would like to thank Andes Press Agency/Carlos Reyes for permission to
reproduce the cover photograph.

The publishers would also like to thank:
Bolsius (UK) Ltd for supplying the candle for the photograph on page 38 and
Christian Art Ltd for the advent calendar in the same photograph; Christian Aid for
the Cafédirect poster on page 37 which is from a set of posters on fair trade, 1993.

The publishers have made every effort to trace the copyright holders, but if they have
inadvertently overlooked any, they will be pleased to make the necessary
arrangements at the first opportunity.

Contents

MAP: where the main religions began

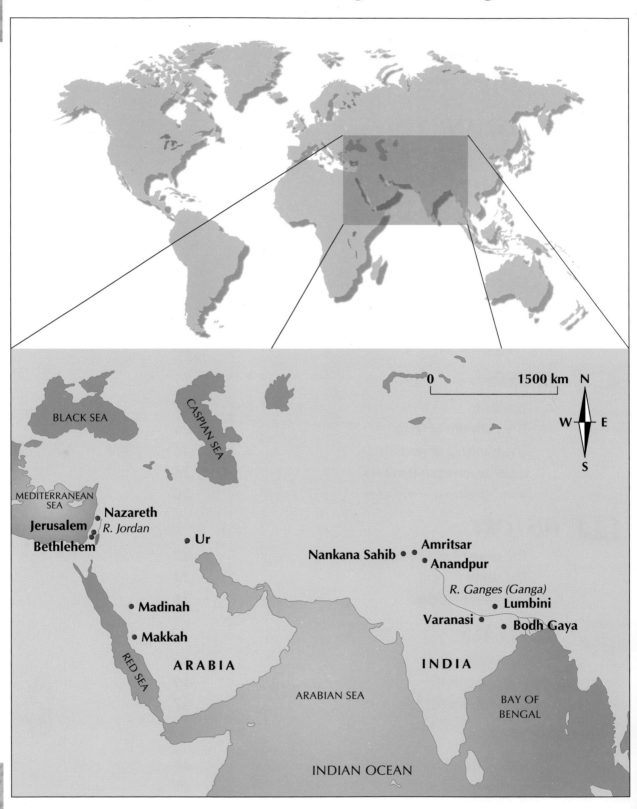

0   1500 km   N

W — E

S

BLACK SEA

CASPIAN SEA

MEDITERRANEAN SEA

Nazareth
Jerusalem *R. Jordan*
Bethlehem

Ur

Nankana Sahib **Amritsar**
Anandpur

R. Ganges (Ganga)

Madinah

Lumbini

Varanasi **Bodh Gaya**

Makkah

RED SEA

ARABIA

INDIA

ARABIAN SEA

BAY OF BENGAL

INDIAN OCEAN

TIME CHART: when the main religions began

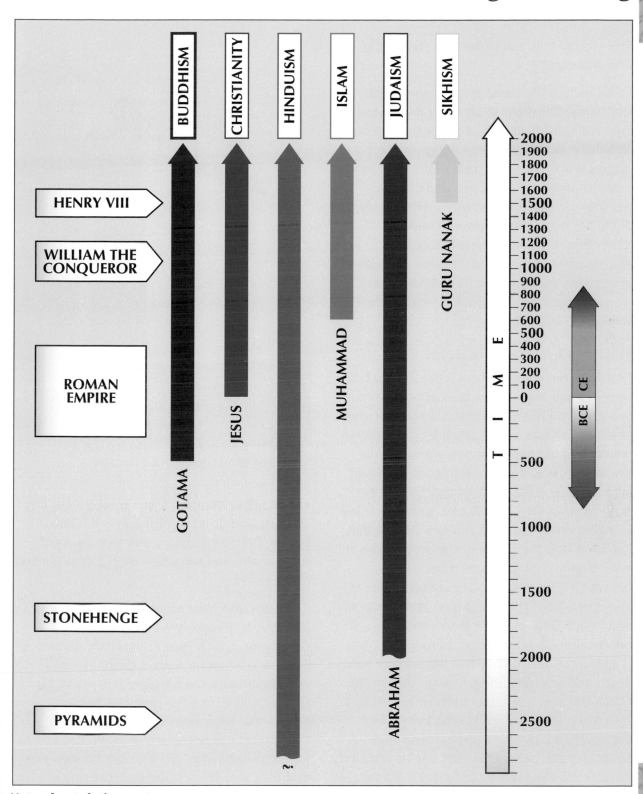

Note about dating systems

In this book dates are not called BC and AD which is the Christian dating system. The letters BCE and CE are used instead. BCE stands for 'Before the Common Era' and CE stands for 'Common Era'. BCE and CE can be used by people of all religions, Christians too. The year numbers are not changed.

Introducing Christianity

This section tells you something about who Christians are.

Christianity is the name given to the religion of Christians. Christians share many beliefs, but they are individuals and of course they do not all believe exactly the same things. Some groups think that some parts of the religion are more important than others, and Christian worship can take place in many different ways. There are two main groups of Christians. 'Orthodox' Christians come mainly from eastern parts of the world. Western Christianity, as its name suggests, has most followers in western countries. This book is mainly about Western Christianity.

What do Christians believe?

Christians believe that there is one God, who is seen in three ways – God the Father, God the Son and God the Holy Spirit. They believe that God the Son was a man called Jesus, who lived on earth about two thousand years ago. For Christians, Jesus is the most important person who has ever lived, because they believe he showed what God is really like. Jesus was killed by being **crucified**, but Christians believe that two days later he rose from the dead, and is still alive, though not in a human body. They believe that his death and **resurrection** are very important. For Christians, Jesus' death showed how much God loves the world, and they believe that his resurrection is proof that there is a life after death. They also believe that Jesus' death and resurrection opened up the way to God – the way which had been closed off by all the wrong things which human beings had done. This is why Christians call Jesus their Saviour – they believe that because he died it is possible for their **sins** to be forgiven. Sins are things that people have done wrong themselves, but sin also includes the idea that

The cross is a symbol of Christianity

everyone has things in their life which cut them off from God, just because they are human beings. Christians also believe that Jesus will come again, and will judge everyone at the end of the world.

Christians take their name from the title which they give to Jesus – 'the Christ'. Christ is a Greek word which means '**Messiah**'. Jesus was a Jew, and when he was on earth, the Jews were waiting for the Messiah who would be sent by God to free the people. Christians believe that Jesus was this Messiah. They believe that it is important to love Jesus, and to follow his teachings. Jesus taught his followers that they should love God and love one another. ('Love' used in this way means 'care for and respect'.)

The beliefs of Christians are summed up in **creeds**. 'Creed' comes from a Latin word which means 'belief'. Two of the most important creeds are the Apostles' Creed and the Nicene Creed. The Nicene Creed is used by Christians all over the world. It is quite long, but it begins:

We believe in one God, the Father, the Almighty, maker of heaven and earth, of all that is, seen and unseen. We believe in one Lord, Jesus Christ, the only Son of God.

Christian symbols

The **symbol** which Christians use most often is a cross. This is because they believe that Jesus' death on a cross was so important. Sometimes the cross has the figure of Jesus on it, and is then called a crucifix.

The other symbol often used by Christians is a fish. This is a sort of code. In the Greek language, the word for fish spells the first letters of the words which mean 'Jesus Christ, God's son, Saviour'. A fish is the symbol for the most important things which Christians believe.

New words

Creed statement of belief
Crucify kill by fastening to a cross
Messiah person to be sent by God to free the Jews
Resurrection returning to life
Sin wrong-doing – something which separates a person from God
Symbol something which stands for something else

Test yourself

What's the resurrection?

What's a crucifix?

What's a creed?

Things to do

1 From the information here, describe as carefully as you can what Christians believe.

2 Why is Jesus called 'Christ'?

3 Explain what Christians mean when they call Jesus 'Saviour'.

4 Draw the two symbols which Christians use most often. For each, say why Christians use it.

This altar cover shows the fish symbol

The Roman Catholic Church

This section tells you about the oldest group in Western Christianity.

After Jesus' death and resurrection, his followers began to tell other people about him, and gradually Christianity became a new religion. The people were called 'Followers of the Way', because they followed the way which Jesus had taught them to live. Everyone who followed Jesus belonged to the same group.

As years passed and the religion developed, there were disagreements over what people should believe. Groups began to split away from each other to form different **Churches**. 'Church' really means a group of Christians who worship together, although it is often used to mean the building where this worship takes place. The most important break in the history of Christianity was in 1054 CE, when the Eastern Church (now called Orthodox) and the Western Church split apart. The Western Church became what we now call the Roman Catholic Church.

Pope John Paul II

The Roman Catholic Church

The Roman Catholic Church is the oldest branch of Western Christianity. It is also the largest. About half of all Christians in the world today are Roman Catholic. Roman Catholics believe that the most important person in the Church is the Pope. 'Pope' comes from a word which means 'father', and so the Pope is the Father of the Church. He is the head of the Church, and he has a special authority. Roman Catholics claim that the line of Popes can be traced back to St Peter, who was one of Jesus' first followers.

Roman Catholics give a special place in their worship to the Virgin Mary, the mother of Jesus. They do not worship her, but they think that she is very important, because she was the mother of Jesus when he was alive on earth. They often pray to her, calling her 'Our Lady', and have a great deal of affection for her. They also pray to **saints**, because they believe that this makes it more likely that God will answer their prayer.

The buildings where Roman Catholics worship usually have statues of the Virgin Mary and of the saints. The statues are not worshipped, but Roman Catholics feel that they help people to concentrate. Often, people who are praying to a saint will light a candle in front of their statue. **Rosary beads** are often used to help people pray, too. A rosary is a special group of prayers. Each of the beads on the string is a reminder of one of these prayers.

Churches usually have people who are specially trained to lead worship and help the people with their lives as Christians. These people are called the **clergy**. A Roman Catholic clergyman is called a **priest**, senior priests are called **bishops**. (These titles are used by other churches, too.) Priests are important to Roman

A statue of the Virgin Mary with Jesus

Praying with rosary beads

Catholics, because they believe that the priest is the link between the people and God. Women are not allowed to become priests, and priests are not allowed to marry, so that they can concentrate on their work without responsibilities to a family.

Priests also hear **Confessions**. Roman Catholics are expected to go to Confession at least once a year. The confessor tells the priest all the things they have done wrong, and the priest tells him or her what to do to show that they are sorry. This usually involves special prayers. A priest must never tell anyone what he has been told in Confession.

New words

Bishop senior member of the clergy

Church group of Christians (also the building where they worship)

Clergy specially trained Christians who are priests, vicars or ministers

Confession admitting something you have done wrong

Priest member of the clergy (often Roman Catholic)

Rosary beads string of beads used as a reminder of prayers

Saint someone who was very close to God when they were alive

Test yourself

What's a church?

What's a saint?

What are rosary beads?

Things to do

1 Explain why the Virgin Mary has a special place in Roman Catholic worship.

2 Why do you think people find it helpful to pray in front of a candle or statue?

3 Why do you think people began the idea of telling a priest all the things they had done wrong? What advantages and disadvantages can you think of?

4 If possible, talk to a Roman Catholic priest about his work. If this is not possible, find out as much as you can about Roman Catholicism from books in the library, and write a short article called 'The Roman Catholic Church'.

The Orthodox Church

This section tells you something about the Orthodox Church.

Christianity did not begin with a complete set of beliefs. Christians had to work out what they believed, and what their beliefs meant to the way they lived. For example, the first followers of Jesus were all Jews, who believed in one God. How did their new belief that Jesus was God's son fit into this? Had he become God's son? Had he always been there? Was he really God? Was he really human? These and many other questions were very important as the new faith developed, and of course different people had different ideas about what the answers should be. Discussions and arguments went on for years – in some cases, they still do.

As the discussions went on, it became clear that two 'camps' were developing. One of these was based in Rome, the other in Constantinople. Gradually the answers which the two groups were providing to important questions became more and more different. Letters between their leaders became more and more bitter. At last, in 1054 CE, the two groups split apart. The Western Church, based in Rome, became the Roman Catholic Church. The Eastern Church, based in Constantinople, became the Orthodox Church.

The Orthodox Church

Today, there are many different branches of Orthodox Christianity. The two largest groups are Russian Orthodox and Greek Orthodox. Most Orthodox Christians live in eastern parts of the world, but there are many thousands of Orthodox Christians living in Europe and America. They share the most important parts of their beliefs with Western Christians but there are many differences between the two.

One difference is that the two churches use different calendars. Although they both celebrate Christmas (see page 38) and Easter (see page 40) as the two most important festivals of the Christian year, they may be celebrated at different times. In the West and in the Greek Orthodox Church, Jesus' birth is celebrated on 25 December. In the Russian Orthodox Church, it is celebrated on 6 January. Easter is a spring festival when Christians celebrate Jesus' death and resurrection. It does not have a fixed date, because it depends on the Spring Equinox. It often happens that in

Inside an Orthodox church in Russia

Icons are painted with great care

the Eastern calendar, Easter falls five weeks later than the Western date. These differences are because of changes that were made in the western calendar in the sixteenth century.

Services in an Orthodox church are led by a priest. There are usually no seats, because the people who have come to worship do not sit down, but stand for the service. A choir leads the singing, but there are usually no musical instruments. An Orthodox church is divided by a screen which hides the **altar**. In the centre of this screen is a pair of doors. Only the priest goes through these doors, but during a service they are opened. This is a symbol which shows that through Jesus it is possible to reach God.

An important part of worship in an Orthodox church is the use of **icons**. An icon is a picture of Jesus, the Virgin Mary or one of the saints. They are beautifully and carefully painted, and many are very old and valuable. Orthodox Christians believe that looking at pictures like these help them to worship. When someone goes into an Orthodox church, the first thing they do is buy a candle, which they light and place in front of an icon. Then they kiss the icon, and make the sign of the cross.

Worship in Orthodox Churches is based on the **liturgy** – written forms of service which go back hundreds of years. Different forms of liturgy are used at different services. The one used most often is the Liturgy of St John Chrysostom.

Test yourself

When did the two groups of Christians split apart?

What's an icon?

What's the liturgy?

Things to do

1 Explain as carefully as you can why the split between the Eastern and Western Churches happened.

2 Using the picture and the text to help you, describe what you would expect to see in an Orthodox church.

3 Explain why icons are so important to Orthodox Christians.

4 Try to find out more about the Russian or Greek Orthodox Church. There may be specialist books in your local library which will give you information, and so will books on church history and encyclopaedias. Work in groups, and put your work together to form a wall-display.

The Protestant Churches

This section tells you about some of the Churches in Western Christianity.

The Protestant Churches are the Churches in Western Christianity which are not Roman Catholic. The word 'Protestant' comes from the sixteenth century, when some people 'protested' about things which they felt were wrong in the Roman Catholic Church at the time. The first Protestants split away from the Roman Catholic Church, and began worshipping on their own. Since that time, there have been many other splits as groups of people disagreed with some of what their own Church was teaching, and broke away to form a new Church. Sometimes groups have joined together to make new Churches, too.

The different branches of Christianity are called **denominations**. There are many different denominations within the Protestant group of Churches. The smallest have only a few churches, the largest have millions of members all over the world. Although some have teachings which are different from all the others, the biggest differences between denominations are usually in the way the Churches are organized, and in how they worship. It is important to remember that even small differences may matter to the people involved, because religion is a major part of the lives of people who believe.

The Anglican Church

The Anglican Church has branches all over the world. In the UK, it includes the Church of England, the Episcopal Church in Scotland, the Church in Wales and the Church of Ireland. The Church of England is the mother Church for all Anglican Churches, although they are not governed by it. The Church of England is 'Established' – which means it is seen as having a special part to play in the way the country is run, and because of this the head of the Church is the Queen. Its clergy have several titles, but most are called **vicars**. The senior clergy are called bishops. The most important bishop is the Archbishop of Canterbury.

Most Anglican churches do not have statues, although they are **dedicated** to one or more saints. Most Anglicans do not pray to the saints or to the Virgin Mary.

The Free Churches

'Free Church' is the group name for most other Protestant Churches. It includes the Methodist, United Reformed and Baptist Churches, and the Church of Scotland. They are called 'Free' because they are not Established like the Church of England. When the Churches were starting, especially, this was seen as being very important. Free Churches do not put the same emphasis on liturgy as the Anglican and Roman Catholic Churches. This means that their services tend to be less formal, and do not usually follow an order written in a book. They also differ in the number of times and the way in which they celebrate **Holy Communion**, the most important service for Christians. Although the Free Churches can be grouped together because they have a lot in common, each of the Churches has items of belief which are different from the others.

The Society of Friends

The Society of Friends was begun by a man called George Fox in the sixteenth century. Early followers were seen to tremble with emotion, and so were given the nickname Quakers, which is still often used. Friends do not have clergy, and their worship is quite different from other Christian groups (see page 19). An important part of the beliefs of the Society of Friends is that they work for peace.

A Protestant church service

They believe disagreements should be solved peacefully, and not by fighting.

The Salvation Army

The Salvation Army was begun by a man called William Booth, during the nineteenth century. He saw being a Christian as being like a soldier fighting against evil. Members wear uniforms, and are organized like an army. They spend much of their time working with drunks, drug addicts and people who are homeless.

Independent churches

There are many churches which are not part of one of the larger groups. They are often 'Pentecostal' – that is, they concentrate on the work of the Holy Spirit. Their worship is often very informal, with singing, dancing and clapping, and members are expected to show the Holy Spirit working in their lives.

Other groups

There are many other groups of Christians all over the world which this book does not have room to mention. Most have teachings which are special to their own people. Some groups have beliefs which are not accepted by the main Churches.

Test yourself

What's a denomination?

What's a bishop?

Who began the Salvation Army?

Things to do

1 Explain why the first Protestants were given this name.

2 Why do you think that William Booth described being a Christian as like being a soldier?

3 George Fox began the Society of Friends, John Wesley began the Methodist Church, William Booth began the Salvation Army. Use your school and local library to find out more about one of these men, and write an article about their life and work.

4 Think of as many reasons as you can why there are so many denominations in Christianity. Do a survey of your local area, and see how many churches of different denominations you can find.

Church buildings 1

This section tells you about the places where Christians worship.

A church is the place where Christians meet to worship. Churches are among the most beautiful and impressive buildings in towns and cities all over the world. Each denomination has its own buildings for worship, and they do not all look the same. Even buildings of the same denomination can be quite different. Some are hundreds of years old, some are modern. This section concentrates on the sort of church you are most likely to see in Britain.

Cathedrals

The most important Roman Catholic, Orthodox and Anglican churches are called **cathedrals**. *Cathedra* is a Latin name for the throne on which a bishop sits, so every cathedral is a 'bishop's church'. Most cathedrals are very old and beautifully decorated.

Roman Catholic churches

Roman Catholic churches are usually built in the shape of a cross or a rectangle, but some modern ones are round. They often have a crucifix or statue outside. The statue may be of the Virgin Mary, or of the saint to whom the church is dedicated.

Orthodox churches

Orthodox churches are usually square. The roof has a **dome**. Most Orthodox churches have collections of bells which are rung before and at times during the services.

Anglican churches

Anglican churches in England are often called **parish** churches. 'Parish' is the name used by several denominations to describe the local area. Anglican churches are often built in the shape of a cross, because Jesus died on a cross.

The Roman Catholic cathedral in Liverpool

An Orthodox church in Birmingham

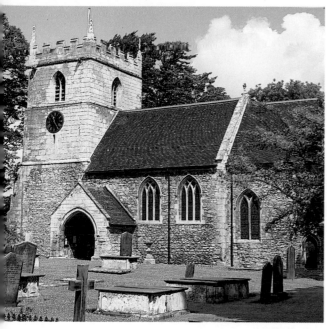

A typical parish church

New words

Cathedral church where a bishop is based
Dome roof shaped like half a ball
Parish local area

Test yourself

What's a cathedral?

What's a dome?

What's a parish?

Things to do

1 Look at the photographs of churches on these pages. What can you tell from their appearance? Write a paragraph about the differences between them.

2 Many churches are very beautifully decorated. How many reasons can you think of why their builders took so much care with their work?

3 Why do most Christians think it is a good idea to have a special building for worship? What are the advantages and disadvantages?

4 Choose one church in your local area. If possible, arrange to go and visit it as a class. If this is not possible, find out as much as you can about it, and do a project with drawings or photographs.

Most have a tower (square) or a spire (pointed). This reminds people to 'look up' to God. Many churches have a clock and bells. This goes back to the days when most people did not have clocks or watches of their own. They needed to be reminded when it was time for services. The bells are also rung for special occasions like weddings and funerals or important events in the life of the country.

Many Anglican churches are very old, and the way they are built can tell you a lot about their history. Rounded arches and thick walls usually mean the building is very old. Thinner, pointed windows and arches are usually more recent.

Free churches

In England, most Free churches were built in the nineteenth century, and are usually quite plain and simple outside. Many Church of Scotland buildings are hundreds of years old, and their appearance usually reflects when they were built. Much depends on the denomination to which the church belongs. For example, many Pentecostal Churches do not have special buildings, but meet in people's homes.

Church buildings II

This section tells you about things you are likely to find inside a church.

All churches are Christian, and so they contain many things which are the same or similar. However, different denominations worship in different ways, and so each church has things which are special to that denomination. As a general guide, Roman Catholic and Orthodox churches usually have most ornaments and decorations, Free churches have fewest.

Altar

The most important part of most churches is a table which is used at the service of Holy Communion. Many Churches call this the altar, Free Churches call it the communion table. It may be made of wood or stone, and is usually at the east end of the building. The area in front of it is called the sanctuary, which means 'holy place'. It is separated from the rest of the church by a rail, called the altar or communion rail. In Orthodox churches, the sanctuary is separated from the rest of the church by a screen called the **iconostasis**, which has icons on it.

In Orthodox and Roman Catholic churches, a special box is kept near the altar. This contains the special bread which is used in Communion.

Lectern

Most churches have a special reading desk which is called the lectern. Lecterns are often very old and are often in the shape of an eagle, though no-one really knows why. A Bible rests on the eagle's wings.

Pulpit

The pulpit is a raised platform at the front of the church. It is usually enclosed, and may be made of wood or stone. The person who is leading the service stands on it to give the **sermon**.

Font

A font is the special bowl used to hold the water for **baptism**. It is often made of stone, and beautifully carved. In many churches the font is near the main door, which is a symbol of

Inside a Roman Catholic church

Fonts are often made of carved stone

A modern stained glass window

baptism being 'entry' to the church. In other churches, it is at the front in the sanctuary. Some churches have a special pool in the floor of the church which is used for baptizing adults (see page 44).

Pews

Many modern churches have ordinary chairs for the people to sit on, but older churches have special benches which are called pews. They face towards the altar, because this is the most important part of the church. Orthodox churches may only have benches around the walls, because the people stand during services.

Statues and icons

Roman Catholic churches usually have statues of saints around the walls. Many older Anglican churches also have them. In an Orthodox church, there are the special pictures called icons. They are used because the people believe that they help them to worship.

Stained glass windows

Many older churches and some modern ones have stained glass in the windows. They help to make the building beautiful. They also go back to the days when many people could not read or write, and the pictures in the windows helped them to understand the Bible stories they were told in church. For the same reason, there may be paintings on the walls in older churches.

New words

Baptism ceremony in which people join the Church
Iconostasis screen which divides an Orthodox church
Sermon special talk which teaches about religion

Test yourself

What's the altar?

What's the lectern?

What's baptism?

Things to do

1 Explain why not all church buildings are exactly the same, even though they are all Christian.

2 Where would you expect to find the font in many churches? Why is this a symbol?

3 Many churches have candles and pictures or icons. Why do you think that people feel this helps them to worship?

4 Draw or make a stained glass window. You could colour it, or cut out an outline and fill it with coloured tissue paper.

Christian worship

This section tells you about how Christians worship.

Christians believe that worshipping God is important. Worship comes from an old word which means 'give worth to' – in other words, showing how much God means to them. Christians praise God, thanking him for everything that he has done, especially for giving his son Jesus to the world, and asking God to be with them in their lives. Worship can take place anywhere, and a Christian does not have to be with anyone else to worship God. However, most Christians believe that worshipping in a group is important, and this is usually called a service. Services in church may be held on any day in the week, but Sunday is a special day, because Christians believe that Jesus rose from the dead on a Sunday.

The Sacraments

Each denomination worships in a different way. The differences between some denominations are very slight, between others they are much more noticeable. Important differences are in the celebration of the **Sacraments**. The Sacraments have been called 'an outward sign of an inward blessing'. For most Christians, they are the most important services, in which they receive blessings from God. However, different denominations have different ideas about what the Sacraments are. For example, the Roman Catholic and Orthodox Churches accept seven Sacraments. Most Protestant Churches accept only two (baptism and Holy Communion), because they believe that these can be traced back to the Bible. The Society of Friends and the Salvation Army do not accept any Sacraments at all, because they do not believe that God is especially present in particular services.

Roman Catholic worship

As they enter the church, many Roman Catholics dip their fingers in the special bowl which is by the door. This is called a **stoup**, and contains water which has been specially blessed by the priest. The person makes the sign of the cross on their forehead, which reminds them of their baptism. Then they bow towards the altar. The most important part of church worship for Catholics is the service called **Mass**, which includes Holy Communion. Like many other churches, Roman Catholic services include hymns, prayers, readings and a sermon. A Roman Catholic service book is called a **missal**.

Orthodox worship

Orthodox church services are sung, but there are no musical instruments – the singing is unaccompanied. **Incense** is used, and there are set prayers and Bible readings for different services. A prayer which Orthodox Christians think is very important is the Jesus prayer – 'Lord Jesus Christ, Son of God, have mercy on me.' The people usually stand for the whole service, which is often longer than a Western service, but it is not unusual for people to move around and arrive or leave whilst it is going on.

Anglican worship

Anglican worship is not the same in every church. Some Anglican churches have services very like Roman Catholic worship. Others are much more like Free Church services. Much depends on the vicar and what the people are comfortable with. In a typical Anglican church service, the worshipper will bow towards the altar as he or she enters the church, then kneel and pray for a few moments. The service includes Bible readings, prayers and the singing of hymns, and there may be chanting (a special sort of singing) led by a choir. Each Church has

A Society of Friends meeting in Chester

its own service book – for example, in the Church of England, most of the service follows the pattern set out in the *Alternative Service Book* or (the older version) the *Book of Common Prayer*. The most important part of the service is the sermon by the vicar. The sermon usually explains some of Jesus' teaching and shows how it has meaning for the lives of the people.

Free Church worship

Worship in the Free Churches does not usually follow anything written in a book, although special services like Holy Communion may be written down. The usual pattern is for hymns, prayers, readings and a sermon. Worship generally is simpler than in other churches. The simplest worship is the meetings (they do not call them services) of the Society of Friends. They do not have clergy, and their meetings are silent until someone feels that God has given them something to say. Salvation Army meetings are often held out of doors so that more people may hear about God. They have bands and joyful singing. Meetings include the opportunity for people who are not Christians to ask God for help and become Christians. Pentecostal services often include singing and dancing. If someone needs help, there will be a 'laying on of hands' where the person is prayed for and blessed. Other people may tell what God has done in their lives.

New words

Incense spice which gives a sweet smell when burned

Mass most important Roman Catholic service

Missal Roman Catholic service book

Sacrament one of a number of services in which Christians believe they are especially blessed

Stoup container for holy water

Test yourself

What's a missal?

What's a sacrament?

What's the Jesus prayer?

Things to do

1 Why do Christians meet for worship on a Sunday?

2 What things are normally included in Christian worship?

3 Write a brief guide to the sort of service you would find in different Churches. What sort of service do you think you would prefer? Why?

4 Design a cover which could be used for a service book. (You could include Christian symbols.)

The Eucharist

A Roman Catholic Mass – blessing the wafer

This section tells you about an important Christian service.

For most Christians, the Eucharist is the most important service. *Eucharist* is a Greek word which means 'thanksgiving'. It is a service in which Christians remember the last meal which Jesus ate with his **disciples** on the night before he was crucified. As part of this meal, Jesus gave his friends bread and wine which he said had a special meaning. They were symbols of his death. The bread was a symbol of his body, which would soon be 'broken' on the cross. The wine was a symbol of his blood. Jesus knew that his death would be a **sacrifice**. He wanted his followers to know this too.

'Eucharist' is only one name for the service. It has several other names. In many Churches, it is called Holy Communion. In the Roman Catholic Church, it is called Mass. In many Free Churches, it is called the Lord's Supper.

In the Church of England, Communion is held at least every Sunday, sometimes more often. The service begins with prayers thanking God for his goodness and for the fact that the people can celebrate in this way. The priest who is leading the service reads a prayer which includes a reminder of why Christians celebrate Holy Communion:

> *The Lord Jesus Christ, in the same night that he was betrayed, took bread and gave you thanks; he broke it and gave it to his disciples, saying 'Take, eat, this is my body, which is given for you; do this in remembrance of me.' In the same way after supper, he took the cup, and gave you thanks; he gave it to them saying 'This is my blood of the new covenant shed for you and for many, for the forgiveness of sins. Do this as often as you drink it, in remembrance of me.'*

The people repeat their beliefs about Jesus: 'Christ has died! Christ is risen! Christ will come again!' then they are invited to eat the bread and drink the wine. They go forward to the altar rail, and are given a piece of bread or sometimes a small round wafer and a sip of wine. The priest says, 'The body of Christ' and, 'The blood of Christ', and the people reply, 'Amen'. The service ends with prayers thanking God that the people have been able to take part in the service, and asking for his help in their lives.

The pattern of the service is similar in other Churches, but each Church is slightly different. For example, in the Roman Catholic Church, it is the main service, and is usually held every day. Roman Catholics normally use special wafers instead of bread. The service of the Eucharist in the Orthodox Churches is set out in the Liturgy, and different liturgies are used depending on the occasion. One difference in the way that the service is celebrated by Orthodox Christians is that the people are given the bread and wine on a spoon. **Fasting** before receiving Communion is very important for Orthodox Christians, and other Christians may choose to fast, too.

Orthodox Christians receive Communion from a spoon.

Free Churches do not hold Communion services as often – sometimes once a month, sometimes less often. For example, in the Church of Scotland it is usually held only four times a year. They believe that this helps to keep the service special. Many Free Churches use fruit juice or non-alcoholic wine which is usually given to the people in individual glasses. In many Free Churches, the people stay in their seats, and the bread and wine are brought to them, to show that everyone is equal in front of God.

Whatever name their Church uses for the service, receiving the bread and wine at Communion is something which is very important to Christians. They believe that the bread and wine are special because they have been blessed, and that by taking part in the service they are following what Jesus told his followers to do. The Communion Service means sharing something special together.

An Anglican Communion service

New words

Disciple pupil – one of Jesus' closest followers

Fast do without food and drink for religious reasons

Sacrifice symbolic offering made to a god

Test yourself

What does 'Eucharist' mean?

What's a sacrifice?

What does fasting mean?

Things to do

1 Explain what Christians believe that the bread and wine symbolize.

2 Why do you think that a service which celebrates Jesus' death is called 'thanksgiving'?

3 What reasons can you think of why Orthodox Christians might use a spoon in the Eucharist service?

4 Read the account of the Last Supper in the Bible. It's in Mark's Gospel, chapter 14 verses 22–26. Write your own account of the meal, explaining why Christians believe that it was so important.

The Bible

This section tells you about the Bible, which is the Christians' holy book.

The Bible is a collection of books which have been put together. It can be divided into two sections. These are called the Old Testament and the New Testament. The Old Testament is more or less the same as the Jewish Scriptures. Jesus was a Jew, so were all his first followers, and some of the beliefs of Jews and Christians are very similar. The New Testament contains stories about the life of Jesus, and other writings from the early days of Christianity.

The Old Testament

The books of the Old Testament can be divided into four main groups. These are books of teaching, of history, of poetry and of **prophecy**. The books show how Jews gradually came to learn more and more about what God is like. Christians believe that Jesus was the way in which God finally showed what he was like. They believe that the Old Testament looks forward to the coming of Jesus. Jews, of course, do not accept this.

The New Testament: Gospels

The first part of the New Testament is made up of the four **Gospels**. This comes from an old word which means 'good news'. They contain stories about Jesus, and things that happened in his life. The men who wrote them were not trying to write the complete story of his life. They were explaining why they believed that Jesus was so important. This explains why the Gospels do not – for example – include anything about what Jesus looked like. The Gospel-writers were interested in the things Jesus said and did, more than anything else. Much of the Gospels are about the last week of Jesus' life, because the writers believed that this was most important. The first three Gospels (Matthew, Mark and Luke) are quite similar. John's Gospel was probably written later, and is written in quite a different way.

The New Testament: The Acts of the Apostles

Apostle is a name given to some of the early Christian preachers. Most – but not all – of the Apostles had been friends of Jesus when he was preaching in Palestine. The Book of Acts tells the story of some of the events in the early days of Christianity. It was probably written by the same person who wrote Luke's Gospel. Much of the Book of Acts is about the journeys made by St Paul, preaching to people about Jesus.

The books that make up the Bible

A decorated capital letter in an old handwritten Bible (15 century CE)

The New Testament: letters

Most of the letters in the New Testament were written by St Paul to groups of Christian friends in different places. They contain advice about being a Christian, and how Christians should live. They have been kept because so much of the teaching is important to every Christian.

The New Testament: Revelation

The last book is the book of Revelation. It is quite different from everything else in the New Testament. One reason for this is that part of the book is written in a sort of code. It was written to encourage people who were being **persecuted** because they were Christians.

How the Bible is used

The Bible is read in church services, and preaching in church is usually based on what the Bible teaches. Christians also read and study it at home. Many Christians meet regularly for Bible study, where a group will discuss a story or passage from the Bible and talk about what it means and how it should affect their lives. Christians believe that knowing what the Bible teaches is an important part of their religion.

New words

Apostles first Christian preachers
Gospels first four books of the New Testament
Persecution ill-treatment because of religion
Prophecy messages from God

Test yourself

What are the two main parts of the Bible?

What are the accounts of Jesus' life called?

Who were the Apostles?

What's persecution?

Things to do

1 The Bible has been called a 'library'. How many reasons can you think of to explain this?

2 Explain why the first part of the Christian Bible is the same as the Jewish Scriptures.

3 Why do you think that the accounts of Jesus' life are called 'good news'?

4 Explain why Paul's letters are part of the Bible.

5 Many old Bibles were beautifully decorated. Look at the example on this page, and write out the names of the Gospels in the same way.

The early life of Jesus

This section tells you about the first part of Jesus' life.

Christians follow the teachings of a man called Jesus. Jesus was a Jew who lived in the first century CE. He came from the country which today we call Israel. In those days it was called Palestine, and was part of the Roman Empire. Most of the information which we have about Jesus' life was collected together and written down by people who were his followers. It is contained in the four Gospels, the first part of the New Testament. Even when information is put together from all the Gospels, it does not give a complete record of Jesus' life. The Gospel writers did not intend to do this, because they were more interested in his teaching, and in showing why they believed he was such a special person.

The birth of Jesus

Luke's Gospel has most detail about the birth of Jesus. Luke says that Jesus was born in Bethlehem, a small town near Jerusalem. His parents were living in Nazareth, a town about 100 kilometres to the north, but they had had to travel to Bethlehem to be included in a Roman census (a count of the population). Luke makes it clear that Jesus was not an ordinary baby. Jesus' mother, Mary, had been told by an angel that she would have a baby whom she should call Jesus. He would be the Son of God. Shepherds were told by angels that the baby had been born, and came to visit him. Matthew's Gospel tells that wise men travelled hundreds of kilometres guided by a new star which their studies told them meant that a king had been born. Matthew also includes in his Gospel the story of how the king, Herod, was told about the birth of a new king by the wise men, and ordered the death of all baby boys in Bethlehem because he wanted to get rid of a possible rival. Mary and her husband Joseph escaped to Egypt with Jesus, and lived there for many years before returning to Nazareth.

The childhood of Jesus

There is only one story in the Gospels about the childhood of Jesus. Luke tells that when Jesus was twelve, he went to Jerusalem with Mary and Joseph for the Jewish Feast of Passover. When they came to return home, Jesus was not with the group. Mary and Joseph spent three days searching for him before they found him in the Temple, the most important building in the Jewish religion. Jesus was talking to the leaders of the religion, who were amazed at his understanding of the Jewish holy books. When Mary asked if he had not realized that they would be worried about him, Jesus said, 'Didn't you know that I would be in my father's house?' This shows that even as a child Jesus felt that his relationship with God was special.

The baptism of Jesus

Nothing else is known about Jesus until he reached the age of about 30. A man known as

Medieval stained glass window showing the escape to Egypt

Jesus was baptized in the River Jordan

'devil' is a way of describing the force of evil in the world, rather than a person. The three temptations were all about the different ways which Jesus could choose to do the work which God wanted him to do. By the time he had spent 40 days in the desert, he knew how God wanted him to act. He was ready to start his work of preaching and teaching – what Christians call his **ministry**.

John the Baptist had begun teaching and baptizing Jews. He told them that he was just a messenger, and that someone would come after him who would be a far better person. John said, 'I am not even good enough to untie his sandals.' As John was preaching one day, Jesus went to him and asked to be baptized. The Bible makes it clear that John knew that this was the person he had been waiting for. He baptized Jesus, and Mark's Gospel says that God's Spirit came down like a dove, and a voice from heaven said, 'You are my own dear son, I am pleased with you.' Mark does not say that anyone apart from Jesus heard or saw this, and it probably means that Jesus was now sure about the work that God wanted him to do.

The temptations

After he had been baptized, Jesus went into the desert. He needed to be alone to think and to pray about the work he was going to do. The Bible says that during this time Jesus was tempted by the devil three times. When the Gospels were written, the idea of a 'devil' was quite common. Many people today think that

New word

Ministry Jesus' preaching and teaching

Test yourself

Why was Jesus born in Bethlehem?

How old was Jesus when he began preaching?

What is Jesus' ministry?

Things to do

1 Look up the accounts of Jesus' birth in the Bible. (Matthew's Gospel chapters 1 and 2, and Luke's Gospel chapter 2). Write your own version of the story.

2 Why did the Gospel writers not include all the details of Jesus' life?

3 How do the Gospel writers make it clear that Jesus' baptism was an important experience?

4 Explain why Jesus needed to spend time alone before he began his preaching.

The ministry of Jesus

This section tells you about Jesus' work and about his death.

After his baptism, Jesus spent about three years teaching and preaching. He spent most of this time in the area of northern Palestine called Galilee, but the Bible suggests that he went to Jerusalem at least once. He collected together a group of followers, who are often called the disciples. The disciples who were closest to Jesus were Peter, James and John. Although there were twelve disciples who were his main followers, it is clear from the Bible that many other people – men and women – spent time with Jesus when they could.

During the three years that he was preaching, Jesus annoyed the leaders of the country in many ways. He did not say the things which they thought he should be saying. Sometimes he said the opposite! He was popular with ordinary people, and his friends included many people who were not thought suitable company for a religious teacher. This meant that some people felt that Jesus was dangerous. Things came to a head when Jesus went to Jerusalem for the Feast of Passover, an important Jewish festival. In those days, the Jews were hoping for a Messiah who would come to free them from the rule of the Romans, whom they hated. Many people thought that Jesus was this Messiah, and as he entered Jerusalem, riding on a donkey, a large crowd gathered. They put their cloaks on the ground in front of him as a sign of respect and waved palm branches, shouting, 'Blessed is the One who comes in the name of the Lord.'

For three days after this, Jesus taught in the Temple, whilst the authorities waited for a chance to arrest him. They did not dare risk doing this publicly. On the Thursday, he ate the Passover meal with his disciples. This was the last meal which he ate with them, and so it is often called the Last Supper. It is the meal which Christians remember in the service of the Eucharist. During the meal, Jesus gave the disciples bread and wine which he said were symbols of his body and blood. He also told them that he had a new commandment which they should obey. They were to love each other, as Jesus had loved them. ('Love' used in this sense means 'care for'.) Christians believe that this is very important.

After the meal had ended, Jesus went with his disciples to a place called the Garden of Gethsemane. There he was arrested. He was taken before the **Sanhedrin**, the court of the Jewish religion. They found him guilty of **blasphemy**, because he would not deny that he was the Son of God. The punishment for blasphemy was death, but the Jewish leaders could not order his killing because Palestine was ruled by the Romans. So Jesus was taken in front of the Roman Governor, a man called Pontius Pilate. The leaders felt that Pilate was not going to be very interested in a charge of blasphemy, because he was not a Jew, so they added another charge, that Jesus 'called himself a king'. As the Roman Governor, Pilate could not ignore this threat, and he ordered that Jesus should be killed.

The standard Roman method of killing was crucifixion, which meant being nailed (or sometimes tied) to a wooden cross. It is one of the most cruel ways of killing which has ever been known. Jesus was crucified on the Friday morning, on a hill just outside Jerusalem. He died in the afternoon, and his followers were given permission to take his body off the cross and bury it. This had to be done quickly, because the Jewish Sabbath began at sunset. On the Sabbath, no work is allowed, and carrying anything is forbidden. Jesus' body was

One artist's idea of the crucifixion

buried in a rock tomb, and the entrance was sealed with a big stone. The Bible makes it clear that the disciples were sure that this was the end of everything they had hoped for.

On the Sunday morning, two of Jesus' women followers went to the tomb to **anoint** his body. This was a normal Jewish custom when someone died, but there had not been time to do it before the Sabbath began. When they got to the tomb, the stone had been removed, and they were met by two men wearing white who told them that Jesus was not there because he had risen from the dead. This is called the Resurrection. The women rushed off to tell the

disciples that Jesus was alive. During the next six weeks, the disciples saw Jesus several times.

No-one really understands what happened at the Resurrection. It is clear from the Bible that after this Jesus did not have a normal human body, because he could go through locked doors and be in more than one place at the same time, but he also ate and drank with the disciples to prove that he was not a ghost. Christians believe that nothing like the Resurrection has happened before or since.

Test yourself

What's blasphemy?

What was the Sanhedrin?

When was Jesus crucified?

Things to do

1 Why do you think that many of the people in authority did not like Jesus?

2 Explain what the people were hoping Jesus would do when he went to Jerusalem.

3 What do you think happened at the Resurrection? Write a brief account of your ideas.

4 Working in groups, produce a drama to tell the story of what happened on Easter Sunday morning. (You'll need to include the women, the men at the tomb, the disciples when they hear the news.)

New words

Anoint to rub with oil
Blasphemy speaking against God
Sanhedrin most important Jewish court

Jesus' teaching – parables

This section tells you about some of the stories which Jesus told.

Jesus spent much of his ministry teaching people about God and about how they should live. Stories are interesting to listen to, and so Jesus taught by telling stories which made people think about themselves and their lives. Many of these stories are **parables**, which are stories with a meaning. Many of the parables came about when people in the crowd listening to Jesus preach asked him questions. On one occasion, a man was asking Jesus about the right way to live. Jewish teaching said that you should 'love your neighbour as yourself', so the man asked Jesus, 'Who is my neighbour?' In reply, Jesus told this story.

The Parable of the Good Samaritan

This story is found in Luke's Gospel, chapter 10 verses 25–37.

A man was travelling the lonely road from Jerusalem to Jericho. He was attacked and robbed. The thieves even took his clothes, and left him lying by the side of the road, half-dead. Not long afterwards, a priest was going down

The Parable of the Good Samaritan

the same road. He did not stop to help, but crossed to the other side of the road, and walked on. Then a Levite (an important official in the Temple) came by. He too walked on. Then a Samaritan came by. He stopped, and gave the man 'first aid', then took him to an inn. He even paid for the man to be looked after until he had recovered.

There are two lessons in this story. The two Jews who passed the man did not try to help him because they did not want to risk touching a dead body. According to Jewish teaching, if he had been dead, and they had touched him, this would have made them 'unclean' – far worse than just dirty. They would not have been able to do their jobs in the Temple until they had been through special ceremonies. Jesus was criticizing people who did not put helping others above everything else. His other lesson was in choosing a Samaritan to be the one who helped. To understand why this was important, you need to know that Samaritans and Jews had been enemies for hundreds of years. The Jews looked down on Samaritans, and in return the Samaritans hated the Jews. For the Jews listening to Jesus, a Samaritan would have been the last person they would have expected to help the man. The answer to the question 'Who is my neighbour?' was unpleasantly clear to the people listening – your neighbour is anyone who needs your help, even if it is someone you do not like.

The Parable of the Sower

This story is found in Mark's Gospel, chapter 4 verses 3–20.

Most of Jesus' stories were about things which were part of the lives of the people listening. In those days, most people grew their own food, and they would have known all about the difficulty of getting a good harvest out of the poor soil in Palestine.

A farmer sowed some seed. In those days, seed was sown by hand, and as he threw the seed on the ground, some of it fell on the path. Birds came and ate it. Some seed fell on ground where there was not much soil. It began to grow well, but the hot sun scorched it because the roots were not deep. Some seed fell at the edge of the field among thorns and weeds. It tried to grow, but the weeds choked the young plants. Some of the seed fell on good ground. It grew well, and gave a good crop.

The disciples asked Jesus to explain the lesson in this story. He said that the seed was like his teaching. Some people took no notice, like the seed that was eaten. Some people tried to follow his teaching, but soon gave up, like the seed that had no roots. Other people listened and tried, but problems got in the way and they gave up, like the seed that fell among weeds. Other people took notice and followed his teaching, and it changed their lives. They were like the seed that gave a good crop.

Christians believe that stories like these give lessons which are just as true today as they were for the people Jesus was talking to. They believe that Jesus' teaching is very important, and try to follow it in their lives.

New word

Parable story with a religious meaning

Test yourself

What's a parable?

What question did the Parable of the Good Samaritan answer?

Things to do

1 What were the lessons which Jesus was teaching in the Parable of the Good Samaritan?

2 Explain the symbols which Jesus used in the Parable of the Sower.

3 Why do you think that Christians pay so much attention to the stories which Jesus told?

4 Write your own modern version of the Parable of the Good Samaritan. You will need to choose someone unexpected to be the one who helps!

The Parable of the Sower

Jesus' teaching – miracles

This section tells you about some of Jesus' **miracles**.

The men who wrote the Gospels believed that Jesus was the Son of God. They wanted to show in their writing why they believed this. One way they used was telling the stories of miracles which Jesus had worked. There are about 35 miracle stories in the Gospels, and many other places where the writers mention Jesus working miracles.

What is a miracle?

People use the word 'miracle' in several different ways. For the writers of the Gospels, the miracles were signs. They showed who and what Jesus was and, most important, they showed what the Kingdom of God is really like. Christians believe that Jesus was able to work miracles because he had the power of God. The greatest miracle of all was the Resurrection, so the Christian faith depends on miracles being possible.

The Sea of Galilee today. Many of Jesus' miracles happened in this area

Why did the Gospel writers include miracles?

The main reason why the writers of the Gospels included miracles was because they wanted to show Jesus' power. For example, the story of the calming of the storm shows Jesus' power over nature (Mark 4:35–41) and the story of the healing of the man with an evil spirit (Luke 4:31–36) shows his power over evil. Probably most of all, the writers wanted to show that God's kingdom is really coming – for example, the turning of water into wine (John 2:1–11).

These two stories show how Mark chose to show Jesus' power in different ways.

The healing of the man let down through the roof (Mark 2:2–12)

Jesus was preaching in a house in Capernaum one day when four men arrived carrying a friend who was paralysed. They could not get near the house because there were so many people listening to Jesus, so they climbed up on the roof. Houses in those days were made of baked mud and had flat roofs with stairs outside. They made a hole in the roof that was big enough to let the stretcher through. When the man was let down in front of him, Jesus said, 'Your sins are forgiven.' This was because, in those days, people believed that illness was often a punishment for things that a person had done wrong. Some strict Jews who were present began to mutter to each other, asking who Jesus thought he was that he dared to forgive sins, since only God had the power to do that. Jesus heard them and asked whether it was easier to tell the man his sins were forgiven, or to say, 'Get up, pick up your mat and go home!' The man got up and walked away. All the people were amazed.

A mosaic picture of the five loaves and two fish

The feeding of the five thousand (Mark 9:2–17)

The feeding of the five thousand is the only miracle which is reported by all four Gospel writers. There are slight differences – this is how Mark tells the story.

Jesus had been teaching a large crowd all day, and it was getting late. The disciples suggested that he should send the people home, but Jesus told them to find food for them instead. The best they could suggest was a boy in the crowd who had brought a 'packed lunch' with him. Jesus took the five loaves and two small fish, and asked God's blessing on them. Then he told the disciples to divide them amongst the crowd. Everyone ate as much as they wanted, but when they had finished, what was left filled twelve baskets.

Many people have tried to explain Jesus' miracles. Some people believe that they really happened, because Jesus had the power to make things that are 'impossible' happen. Others believe that the stories should be seen as symbols. Some people believe that they can be explained scientifically. To the writers of the Gospels the miracles were signs of Jesus' power. Christians today believe that this power can still be seen at work in the world.

Test yourself

What's a miracle?

How many miracles are there in the Gospels?

Things to do

1 Explain the reasons why the Gospel writers included miracles.

2 Why did the Jews who were present think that Jesus should not tell the man that his sins were forgiven?

3 Imagine that you were a newspaper reporter at one of these miracles. Write a short article describing what you saw. Think up a suitable headline.

4 People often talk today of miracles happening. Work in groups to make a list of things which have been described like this. Discuss whether you think any are the same sort of miracle as in the Bible.

The growth of Christianity

This section tells you about how Christianity developed.

The first followers of Jesus probably had no idea that they would be starting a new religion. It was only gradually, as their ideas developed, that they began to move away from their Jewish background.

The most important change was in the way they treated people who were not Jews. In those days no good Jew would have anything to do with a non-Jew. Gradually, the early Christians began to think that this was wrong. The turning point was a **vision** which Peter had. The story is in the Book of Acts, chapter 10. Peter saw a huge piece of cloth being let down from the sky, full of animals and birds, and a voice told him to kill and eat. Jews have very strict laws about not eating certain foods, and many of the things in the cloth were forbidden. Peter said that he could not possibly eat them, but the voice told him that God had made them, and it was not for him to judge whether or not they were fit to eat. This happened three times. As Peter was struggling to work out what the vision meant, messengers arrived from a Roman soldier called Cornelius. He was not a Jew, but he was very interested in the Jewish faith. He too had had a vision, telling him to send for Peter to come and teach him. Peter understood that the two visions were linked. Just as he had no right to judge what animals on the cloth he should eat, so he had no right to judge who should be taught about Jesus.

After this, Peter began to persuade the other Christians that non-Jews could become followers of Jesus, too. The change was so enormous that there were still many more arguments and discussion, but from this point on, Christianity began to expand out of the Jewish faith. This meant that it could reach many more people.

More than any other person, the man who helped Christianity to spread was Saul of Tarsus. He was a very strict Jew, and when he first heard about the Christians, he was very angry. He thought that it was wrong for any man to be worshipped as the Christians worshipped Jesus. He began persecuting Christians, to try to make them give up their faith. As he travelled to the town of Damascus to find Christians who had gone there, he had a vision in which God told him to stop persecuting Christians. As a result of this vision,

How Christianity spread

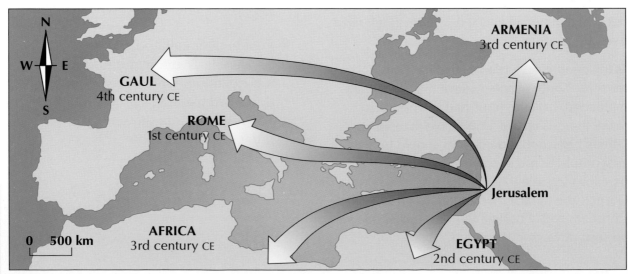

ARMENIA
3rd century CE

GAUL
4th century CE

ROME
1st century CE

Jerusalem

AFRICA
3rd century CE

EGYPT
2nd century CE

0   500 km

This early Christian statue shows Jesus as the Good Shepherd

he changed completely. He changed his name to its Roman form, Paul, and for the rest of his life he travelled all over the Roman Empire preaching to people about Jesus. His life was far from easy, but he said it was all worth it, because he was able to preach about Jesus. Eventually he was killed by the Romans who were persecuting Christians.

The first two hundred years of Christianity were times of great persecution. The Roman Emperors were worshipped as gods, and they did not tolerate religions which not only refused to worship them, but also seemed to be dangerous because they were spreading so fast. Christians all over the Roman Empire suffered and died because of their faith.

Although being a Christian was very difficult, Christianity did not die out. Instead, its numbers grew. This was probably because

New word

Vision dream which includes a religious experience

people who had to fight for what they believed were more likely to convince other people that it was true. Christianity continued to be illegal until 313 CE, when the Emperor Constantine believed that he had been given victory in battle by the Christians' God. He made Christianity a legal religion. Within another hundred years it had become the official religion of the Roman Empire.

Test yourself

What's a vision?

What did Saul change his name to?

When did Christianity become a legal religion?

Things to do

1 Explain carefully what Peter's vision was. Why was it so important for Christianity?

2 Why do you think that Christianity grew so quickly when Christians were being persecuted?

3 What can you tell about being a Christian from Paul's life?

4 Find out more about what it was like to be a Christian in Roman times. Looking in history books and encyclopaedias will help (look up 'Christian persecution' and 'catacombs'). Do a project with drawings as well as written information.

The Saints

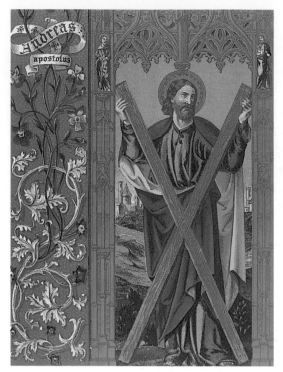

An old painting showing St Andrew

This section tells you about some Christian saints.

Christianity has thousands of saints, from all areas and ages of the religion. A saint is a person who lived an especially good life. Many saints were **martyrs** – people who were killed because of their faith. There are two reasons why saints are given great respect. The first is because they lived such good lives. The second reason is the belief that because saints were so holy when they were alive, they are still special after death. Many Christians (especially Roman Catholics and Orthodox) pray to the saints because they believe this makes it more likely that a prayer will be granted. They hope that the saint will persuade God to listen. The proper name for this is that the saint will **intercede** for them.

One of the best-loved saints is St Francis. He was born in the town of Assisi in Italy in 1181 CE. He was the son of a rich merchant, and could have had a comfortable life, but he felt that God was telling him to live in a very different way. He left home, and chose to live in great poverty – he wore only simple clothes, lived in a mud hut with no furniture and few books, and spent much of his life caring for the poor and sick. He was joined by seven men who shared his view of life, and from this developed the Franciscans, an **Order** of **monks** which still exists today. St Francis is remembered for the holiness of his life, and for the way in which he saw everything in the world as being part of God's creation.

Patron saints

When they prayed to the saints, people gradually came to believe that a particular saint was helping them. This led on to the idea of saints being interested in particular situations, usually because of their job or something they did when they were alive on earth. They are called patron saints, and can be prayed to for special help. For example, St Christopher is the patron saint of people who are travelling. This is because the story of St Christopher's life says that he was a giant called Opher who lived in the third century. His job was to help people to cross a river, and one day a child asked to be carried over. As they crossed, the child became so heavy that Opher could barely carry him. When they got to the other side, the child said that he was Jesus, and that Opher had carried the weight of the sins of the world. He also said that Opher was to change his name from Opher which means 'bearer or carrier' to Christopher, which means 'Christ-bearer'. Many churches have pictures of St Christopher, because a tradition grew up that anyone who saw a picture of him would not die that day. This is also the reason for wearing St Christopher medallions, but for many people now this is more superstition than a religious belief.

Each country has its own patron saint. The four patron saints of the British Isles are Andrew (Scotland), David (Wales), George (England)

and Patrick (Ireland). Each country celebrates their saint in different ways. For example, the flag of Scotland shows St Andrew's cross, a diagonal cross on which he is said to have been crucified. Every saint has a day on which he or she is especially remembered, and there are often special ceremonies in a country to celebrate the patron saint's day. St David's Day is 1 March, St Patrick's Day is 17 March, St George's Day is 23 April, St Andrew's Day is 30 November.

Pilgrimage

For hundreds of years, Christians have gone on **pilgrimages** to special places connected with saints. A pilgrimage is a journey made for religious reasons. The idea of pilgrimage is that getting closer to a saint will make prayers more powerful. It may be a pilgrimage to the place where a saint was born, where they died or where their body (or part of it) is buried. One of the most famous places of pilgrimage in Britain is Canterbury Cathedral, where St Thomas à Becket was murdered in 1170 CE.

This tablet in Canterbury Cathedral marks the place where St Thomas à Becket was murdered

Test yourself

What's a martyr?

What's a patron saint?

What's a pilgrimage?

Things to do

1 Think of as many reasons as you can why many Christians pray to saints as well as to God.

2 Many saints died in horrible ways rather than give up what they believed. Why do you think that they were prepared to do this?

3 Explain why pilgrimage may be important for someone who prays to a saint.

4 Choose three of the saints mentioned in this section. For each one, write a brief story of their life, with a picture to show their special interest.

Christianity today

This section tells you something about Christianity in the world today.

Christianity is the largest religion in the world. There are many different groups and sorts of Christians, but in 1993 about 1800 million people worldwide were counted as having some sort of link with Christianity. All Christians share some beliefs, but there are many different ways of living life as a Christian. Some Christians feel that it is enough just to believe what Jesus taught. At the other extreme, some Christians feel that they need to devote their whole life to their religion.

Nuns and monks

Ever since Christianity began, some Christians have felt that they should dedicate their lives to serving God in a special way. People who choose to do this are often called monks and **nuns**. There are thousands of monks and nuns today, mainly belonging to the Roman Catholic and Orthodox branches of Christianity. Most are members of Orders, which means they live in groups following the same rules. Some Orders are 'enclosed' which means they have as little as possible to do with people outside the Order, so that they can concentrate on prayer and **meditation**. Members of other Orders work 'in the world', for example as teachers or nurses. When they join an Order, all monks and nuns make **vows**, promising to live in a particular way. The three most common vows are that they will own nothing (everything will be provided by the Order), that they will not marry, and that they will obey the head of their Order. Taking these vows means that they do not have to worry about things like where they will live or how they should earn their living. Instead, they are free to concentrate on serving God.

Helping others

Christians believe that every human being was made by and is loved by God. Much of Jesus' teaching makes it very clear how important it is to help other people. In the Parable of the Sheep and the Goats, Jesus said that anything which was done for people in need was done for him. For these reasons, many Christians think that they should spend time helping people who are less fortunate than themselves. This may be their full-time job, or it may be as a volunteer in their spare time. Some groups, like the Salvation Army, work as an organized team, helping people who are homeless or who have drink or drugs problems. Other people work

Nuns and monks work in many different ways

Drink a fair cup of coffee!

These friends drink Cafédirect happily, knowing the pickers of this coffee have decent conditions. It is the first fairly traded supermarket coffee.

Christian Aid

Helping others isn't always hard work!

with groups or as individuals to help look after people in need.

Missionaries

Some Christians feel that they will serve God best by going to work with people in other countries. Someone who travels to another country to preach is called a **missionary**. Missionaries brought Christianity to Britain over 1500 years ago. Particularly during the last century, many missionaries went from Britain just to preach to people about Jesus, and try to persuade them to become Christians. Today, attitudes have changed, and although Christians still go to developing countries to preach they now usually offer practical help as well, for example as engineers or doctors. Many people who want to help in this way work with charities which have a Christian basis like Christian Aid or Tear Fund.

New words

Meditate to think deeply, especially about religion
Missionary someone who travels to preach
Nun woman who has dedicated her life to God
Vows solemn promises

Test yourself

Which Churches do most monks and nuns come from?

What does 'meditate' mean?

What's a vow?

What's a missionary?

Things to do

1 What are the three vows which monks and nuns take? Why do you think they are so important?

2 What advantages and disadvantages can you think of in being a monk or nun?

3 How many reasons can you think of why Christians believe it is important to help other people?

4 Look up the Parable of the Sheep and the Goats. It's in Matthew's Gospel, chapter 25 verses 31–46. Write your own version of the story.

5 See if it is possible to arrange for a speaker from a Christian charity to come and talk about the charity's work.

Celebrations I

This section tells you about important events in the first part of the Christian year.

Advent

The church year begins in December, with the season called 'Advent'. Advent is the four weeks before Christmas. It is the time when Christians look forward to Christmas, when they celebrate the birth of Jesus. They also think about the belief that Jesus will come again to begin a new kingdom on earth.

Advent is a time of hope and preparation. Many Christians use Advent candles and Advent calendars as ways of showing this. Advent candles are marked in sections so that one can be burned each day. Advent calendars usually have a door to open each day. They are ways of showing that Christmas is getting closer and help to show how important it is.

Christmas

The word Christmas comes from 'Christ's mass', the church service held on 25 December to celebrate Jesus' birth. This is not the actual date on which Jesus was born, because no one knows when that was. Long before the time of Jesus, 25 December was a festival day and it was adopted by the Christians. Jesus' birth has been celebrated on this date in the Western church since about 300 CE. Most Orthodox Christians celebrate Christmas on 6 January, because of the difference in calendars. Many Christians go to Midnight Mass on Christmas Eve, or to a service on Christmas Day. They want to thank God for giving his son Jesus to the world. The Bible readings are the Gospel stories about the birth of Jesus, and special hymns called **carols** are sung. The name 'carol' comes from a French word which means 'dance', and hundreds of years ago people used to dance around churches as they were singing.

Christmas has become a national holiday in many parts of the world, and is a special time for many people who are not Christians. It is important to remember that many Christmas customs are not really anything to do with Christianity. Many customs had a religious meaning at first, but this has often been forgotten. For example, Father Christmas as an old man in a long red cloak has nothing to do with Christianity, but his other name, Santa Claus, relates to St Nicholas, the patron saint of children (see page 34). In many countries in Europe, children are given presents on 6 December, which is St Nicholas' Day, rather than at Christmas.

Many ways of celebrating Christmas – for example, Christmas cakes, Christmas dinner – are more to do with tradition than religion. Christians take part in them too, but for Christians the main point of Christmas is to remember that God gave his son Jesus to the world.

An advent calendar and candle

A Christmas crib

Boxing Day

The day after Christmas Day is called Boxing Day. Hundreds of years ago, there were special boxes in churches. Money was collected in them through the year. On Boxing Day they were opened, and the money was given to the poor.

Epiphany

Epiphany in the Western church is on 6 January. It is the end of the twelve days of Christmas. Epiphany means 'showing', and it celebrates the story in Matthew's Gospel about how Jesus was shown to wise men who had travelled to see him, guided by a star. In Orthodox Churches which celebrate Christmas on 6 January, Epiphany is 19 January. Orthodox Christians celebrate Epiphany as the time when Jesus was shown to be the Son of God at his baptism (see page 24).

New word

Carol joyful hymn

Test yourself

When is Advent?

What does the name 'Christmas' come from?

When is Epiphany?

What does 'Epiphany' mean?

Things to do

1 Explain why Jesus' birthday is such an important festival for Christians.

2 Where does the name for Boxing Day come from? Why do you think there was a need to have boxes for the poor?

3 What two things do Christians celebrate at Epiphany?

4 Write a poem which would be suitable to use as a Christmas carol.

Celebrations II

This section tells you about the most important festivals of the Christian year.

Lent

Lent is the most solemn time of the Christian year. It takes place in spring, during the six weeks before Easter. It is the time when Christians remember that Jesus spent time alone in the desert, preparing for his work of preaching and teaching. During Lent, Christians think about how they live their lives.

The day before the beginning of Lent is Shrove Tuesday. 'Shrove' is an old English word which means being forgiven for the things you have done wrong. In olden days, everyone went to Confession (see page 9). This meant that they could have a clean start to the serious time of Lent. It is still a special day for going to Confession in some churches. The other name for Shrove Tuesday is 'Pancake Day'. This is because Lent was a time when everyone fasted – that is, they ate only very plain and simple foods. Pancakes became a traditional way of using up foods like fat and eggs which would go off before Easter. Many Christians still choose to give something up for Lent and, in the Orthodox Church, Lent is still a time of strict fasting.

The first day of Lent is called Ash Wednesday. Its name comes from the special service held on this day. Special ash is used to mark the sign of the cross on a person's forehead. It is a sign that they are really sorry for the things that they have done wrong. This service is still an important one for many Christians, although it is not used in all Churches.

Easter

Easter is the most important and the most joyful Christian festival. Christians remember Jesus' death, and celebrate his resurrection.

Easter eggs are a symbol of new life

The week before Easter is called Holy Week when Christians remember the special events in Jesus' life in the week before his crucifixion (see page 26). It begins on Palm Sunday, when Christians remember that Jesus rode into Jerusalem on a donkey. Maundy Thursday was the day on which Jesus ate the Last Supper with his disciples. Its name comes from the Latin word *mandatum*, which means 'command'. At the meal, Jesus told his friends he was giving them a new commandment.

Good Friday is a very solemn day on which Christians remember that Jesus was crucified. Christians believe that because Jesus died, their sins – everything which human beings do wrong – can be forgiven. They believe that Jesus' death opened up the way to God. This is why it is called 'Good' Friday. Solemn church services are held, especially around 3 o'clock in the afternoon, which the Gospels say is the time Jesus died. Churches are never decorated, and in many churches the altar candles and ornaments are covered with a cloth.

Easter Sunday is the most joyful day of the Christian year. Church services celebrate the belief that Jesus rose out of the tomb and was seen alive by his friends. Christians believe that he is still alive today, although not on earth and

An Orthodox service at Easter

not in a human body. They believe that the Resurrection shows that death is not the end, it is a new beginning of life with God. Most Christians make a special effort to go to a Eucharist service on Easter Day.

In the Orthodox Church, Easter services are especially important. There is a special service at midnight as Easter Day begins. The church is in darkness, to show that Jesus is in the tomb. (One of the titles which Christians give Jesus is the 'Light of the World'.) The priest comes out from behind the centre screen with a lighted candle, and all the people light their candles from his. The church gradually fills with light. This is a symbol that the Light of the World has returned. The people tell each other that 'Christ is Risen!' It is a very joyful time.

Test yourself

When does Lent begin?

What does '*mandatum*' mean?

What happened on Good Friday?

2 Why does the day on which Jesus died have the name 'Good' Friday?

3 How many reasons can you think of why believing in the resurrection of Jesus is so important for Christians?

Things to do

1 Explain why Christians often give up something for Lent.

4 Why do you think Christians call Jesus the 'Light of the World'?

Celebrations III

This section tells you about other important Christian festivals.

Ascension Day (Acts 1:9–11)

Ascension Day is 40 days after Easter. It is the day on which Christians remember the last time that Jesus' disciples saw him on earth. No one really knows what happened on this day, but Jesus' friends knew that they were not going to see him again. The Bible says that 'a cloud hid him from their sight'. Some Christians believe that this means there was a miracle, and Jesus was lifted away from them. Other people believe that Jesus walked up the hill until he was hidden by mist.

Pentecost (Acts 2:1–4)

Before Jesus left his friends, he promised that he would send the Holy Spirit to guide them. Christians believe that the Holy Spirit is part of God – the part which is God's power working in the world. Jesus' disciples were given this power so that they could teach and heal people, just as Jesus had done. The disciples were hiding in a room in Jerusalem when they saw what looked like flames of fire, and heard a noise like a rushing wind. They forgot that they were afraid, and rushed out and began to preach about Jesus to the people outside. Pentecost is therefore often thought of as being the point where Christianity really began. To show how important it is, and how important they believe the Holy Spirit is, many Christians join in processions around their town. This helps to show people that they believe the Holy Spirit is still working in the world today. The other name for Pentecost is Whit Sunday, which goes back to the days when people often joined the church and were baptized on this day, and wore white clothes for the ceremony.

Trinity Sunday

To understand the idea of God as Trinity, you need to understand something of the background of Christianity. All the first Christians were Jews, and they believed very firmly that there was only one God. As the beliefs of Christianity developed, this led to a problem. They believed that there was only one God, but they also believed that Jesus was God. They believed that Jesus was still with them on earth, even though he was no longer in a human body. The answer to how these things are possible is the belief in God as Trinity. Religious thinkers struggled for hundreds of years before the belief in the Trinity was finally settled, because the idea is complicated. 'Tri' means three, so God as Trinity means that the one God can be seen in three ways. These are usually described as God the Father, God the Son and God the Holy Spirit. Christians believe that God is an eternal spirit who never changes. When Jesus was alive on earth he was completely man, but he was also completely God. The Holy Spirit is God at work in the world. Christians therefore believe that the

Many Christians join in processions at Pentecost

Trinity is important because it describes God. They believe that they are *able* to worship because Jesus showed what God is like, and they have the *power* to worship because of the Holy Spirit. On Trinity Sunday, Christians think especially about what God is like, and about their own lives as Christians.

Harvest festival

Harvest festivals were celebrated thousands of years before the time of Jesus, and so they are not just Christian festivals. Most Churches celebrate harvest festivals, usually in late September. Churches are specially decorated with fruit and flowers, because harvest is a time for thanking God for providing food and necessary things in life. In the days when most people were farmers, the harvest festival was a time for thanking God that their harvest had been safely collected. Today, for most people harvest is a symbol of how much everyone depends on each other. In many Churches, the harvest festival is also a time for thinking of Jesus gathering his followers together when he comes back to earth at the end of time to judge everyone.

Test yourself

What do Christians remember on Ascension Day?

What were the disciples given at Pentecost?

What do Christians thank God for at harvest?

Things to do

1 Read the description of the Ascension in the Book of Acts, chapter 1. Then write your own description of what you think happened.

2 Why do Christians believe that Pentecost was so important?

3 Explain carefully how Christians came to believe that God is a Trinity.

4 Make a display called 'Harvest'. You could use objects as well as writing and pictures.

Churches are decorated for harvest festival

Special occasions I

This section tells you about special services held when people join the Church.

Baptism

Baptism is the word used by most Christians for the service in which people join the Church, and are officially given their name. Sometimes the word 'Christening' is used instead. In most denominations, babies are brought to church for the ceremony by their parents, along with friends or relatives who are called godparents. The godparents as well as the parents make promises that the child will be brought up to follow the teachings of Jesus.

Baptism is often part of an ordinary church service. The vicar or minister and the parents and godparents (one of whom usually carries the baby) gather round the font, a special container for water which has been blessed. The priest uses the water to make the sign of the cross on the baby's head, and says, 'I baptize you (baby's name) in the name of the Father, and of the Son and of the Holy Spirit.'

The Baptist Church and many Pentecostal Churches do not baptize babies, because they believe that baptism should wait until a person is

A total immersion baptism

old enough to make promises for themselves. Babies are blessed, but anyone who is baptized is at least in their late teens. The person receives teaching about Christianity, and is then baptized by **total immersion**. This means that their whole body is covered by water. Men wear a white shirt and trousers, women wear a long white dress. The minister wears waders, and goes into a special waist-deep pool in the floor of the church. (Sometimes a local swimming pool or river is used instead.) The person who is being baptized walks down the steps into the pool, and makes a series of promises. These include that they are sorry for the things they have done wrong in the past, and that they believe in Jesus. Then they are carefully submerged by the minister. Usually there are two sets of steps in the pool, and the person leaves by the steps at the opposite end, to show that they are starting a new life.

In the Orthodox Church, babies are also baptized by total immersion. The priest says, 'The servant of God (baby's name) is baptized into the Name of the Father, Amen. And of the Son, Amen. And of the Holy Spirit, Amen.' As

Baptizing a baby

each part of the Trinity is mentioned, the baby is immersed in the font. Immediately after baptism, the baby is **chrismated** – the equivalent of **confirmation**. The priest anoints the baby with oil eight times on different parts of the body, saying, 'The seal of the gift of the Holy Spirit.' After chrismation, children take a full part in Eucharist services.

Christians believe that baptism is a ceremony which washes away sin. This does not just mean wrong things that the person has done themselves (obviously a baby has never done anything wrong). It also includes the things which come between all human beings and God. Baptism is therefore a symbol of the spiritual birth of the person, as well as being the time when they join the Church.

Confirmation

Confirmation is a service held by Churches which baptize babies. In the Roman Catholic Church, **confirmands** are usually seven or eight. In most other Churches, they are at least teenage, but there is no age limit. The service is held so that they can make their own promises about being a Christian. They make again ('confirm') the promises which were made for them when they were baptized. Christians believe that the Holy Spirit is given at confirmation, and the person becomes a full member of the Church. In some Churches, people are not allowed to receive the bread and wine at the Eucharist until they have been confirmed.

In the Anglican and Roman Catholic Churches, confirmation is performed by a bishop. In Free Churches, the equivalent service is usually performed by the church minister. Each confirmand is asked questions about their beliefs, and the bishop lays his hands on their head as he prays for them. In the Roman Catholic Church, the bishop makes the sign of the cross in oil on the person's forehead. At the end of a confirmation service, the person is welcomed as a full member of the Church.

New words

Chrismation service to anoint with oil
Confirmand someone who is going to be confirmed
Confirmation service to confirm baptism promises
Total immersion way of baptizing in which the whole body is submerged

Test yourself

What's baptism?

What's a font?

What's confirmation?

Things to do

1 Explain why water is so important in a baptism service.

2 Why is confirmation a necessary service?

3 How old do you think someone should be before they make promises about what they believe and how they want to live?

4 If possible, ask a member of the local clergy to come and talk to your group about baptism. Remember to prepare some questions first!

Special occasions II

This section tells you what Christians teach about marriage and death.

Marriage

The Bible says that marriage was given to human beings by God, who intended it to join men and women together for life so that they could help each other. Christians do not have to marry in church, but many couples feel that they wish to make their vows there and receive God's blessing. Marriage is different from all other church services, because it is a legal ceremony as well as a religious one. This means that there must be at least two people present as well as the couple and the vicar or minister, and some of the words of the service have to be included by law. The couple and their witnesses must also sign a register, which is a legal document.

In most Western Churches, the marriage service is very similar. The bride and groom state that they do not know any reason why they should not marry each other, and promise that they will love each other and stay together until one of them dies. As a sign of these promises, the groom gives the bride a ring, which she wears on the third finger of her left hand. It is becoming more common for the bride to give the groom a ring, too. After prayers for the couple's life together, the wedding service ends with the signing of the register. Sometimes (especially in the Roman Catholic Church), the service also includes Holy Communion.

In the Orthodox Church, the wedding service is in two parts. In the first part, rings are blessed and exchanged. In the second part, the priest places crowns on the couple's heads. In Greek churches, these are made of leaves and flowers. In Russian churches, they are of silver or gold. They are a symbol of God's blessing on the couple. At the end of the service, the couple drink from the same cup of wine, which is a symbol of their new life together.

Divorce

Christian teaching says that marriage should only end with death. However, all Churches accept that sometimes marriages do break down. Different Churches have different attitudes to what happens after the breakdown of a marriage. The Roman Catholic Church does not accept divorce – the legal ending of a marriage. At most it accepts a separation, which means that the couple remain married, but no longer live together. The Orthodox Church accepts divorce where a marriage has broken down, and allows re-marriage in church, although there is a different service for people who are marrying for a second time. Re-marriage in church is only allowed after the Church has given the couple a divorce, as well as their legal divorce. The Anglican Churches accept divorce, but do not normally allow divorced people to remarry in church. Free Churches accept divorce, and remarriage is sometimes allowed, if the minister feels that the

Bride and groom exchanging wedding rings

couple are really serious about making this marriage work.

Death

Christians believe that death is not the end, it is the beginning of a new life with God. A Christian funeral is therefore a time of hope as well as a time of sadness. Usually there is a service either in church or at a **crematorium**. Cremation is becoming more common. Prayers are said for the person who has died, entrusting their **soul** to God, and asking God to bless the

A Roman Catholic funeral service

person's relatives and friends. After the service, the body is either buried in a cemetery, or taken to be cremated.

After death

Belief in life after death is an important part of Christian teaching. Most Churches teach that the soul lives on, and about a time at the end of the world when Jesus will return as King and Judge. This is usually linked with teachings about an after-life in which those who love God will go to 'Heaven' and those who reject God will go to 'Hell'.

Test yourself

What do the crowns symbolize in an Orthodox wedding?

What's divorce?

What's cremation?

Things to do

1 Why do you think that Christians choose to marry in church? Many people who are not Christian wish to marry in church too – can you explain this?

2 Explain what the attitude of different Churches to divorce is.

3 Why is a Christian funeral a time of hope as well as of sadness?

4 Why do you think there is no fixed teaching about what life after death might be like?

New words

Crematorium place where dead bodies are burned
Soul a person's spirit which survives death

Glossary

Altar special table used for the service of Holy Communion

Anoint to rub with oil

Apostles first Christian preachers

Baptism service in which people join the Church

Bishop senior member of the clergy

Blasphemy speaking against God

Carol joyful hymn

Cathedral church where a bishop is based

Chrismation service to anoint with oil

Church group of Christians (also the building where they worship)

Clergy specially trained people who are priests, vicars or ministers

Confession admitting something you have done wrong

Confirmand someone who is to be confirmed

Confirmation service to confirm baptism promises

Creed statement of belief

Crematorium place where dead bodies are burned

Crucify kill by fastening to a cross

Dedicate to name in honour of

Denomination branch of Christianity

Disciple pupil – one of Jesus' closest followers

Dome roof shaped like half a ball

Fast do without food and drink for religious reasons

Gospels first four books of the New Testament

Holy Communion most important Christian service

Icon image or picture used in worship

Iconostasis screen which divides an Orthodox church

Incense spice which gives a sweet smell when burned

Intercede to speak on someone's behalf

Liturgy written order of service

Martyr someone who is killed for their beliefs

Mass most important Catholic service

Meditate to think deeply, especially about religion

Messiah person to be sent by God to free the Jews

Ministry Jesus' preaching and teaching

Miracle event which shows a power beyond what is normal

Missal Roman Catholic service book

Missionary someone who travels to preach

Monk man who dedicates his life to God

Nun woman who dedicates her life to God

Order group of nuns or monks who live by the same rules

Parable story with a religious meaning

Parish local area

Persecution ill-treatment because of religion

Pilgrimage journey for religious reasons

Priest member of the clergy (often Roman Catholic)

Prophecy messages from God

Resurrection returning to life

Rosary beads string of beads used as a reminder of prayers

Sacrament one of a number of services in which Christians believe they are especially blessed

Sacrifice symbolic offering made to a god

Saint someone who was very close to God when they were alive

Sanhedrin most important Jewish court

Service Christian meeting for worship

Sermon special talk which teaches about religion

Sin wrong-doing – something which separates a person from God

Soul a person's spirit which survives death

Stoup container for holy water

Symbol something which stands for something else

Total immersion way of baptizing in which the whole body is submerged

Vicar member of the Anglican clergy

Vision dream which includes a religious experience

Vows solemn promises